Extreme Readers

CONFIDENT
3
READER

Weird and Wacky Plants

By Katharine Kenah

School Specialty
Publishing
Columbus, Ohio

School Specialty Publishing

Copyright © 2005 School Specialty Publishing, a member of the School Specialty Family.

Printed in the United States of America. All rights reserved. Except as permitted under the United States Copyright Act, no part of this publication may be reproduced or distributed in any form or by any means, or stored in a database or retrieval system, without prior written permission from the publisher, unless otherwise indicated.

The publisher would like to thank the NOAA Photo Library, NOAA National Estuarine Research Reserve Collection; Waquoit Bay, Massachusetts and Alison Robb for their permission to reproduce their photograph used on page 12 of this publication.

Library of Congress Cataloging-in-Publication Data is on file with the publisher.

Send all inquiries to:
School Specialty Publishing
8720 Orion Place
Columbus, OH 43240-2111

ISBN 0-7696-3184-3

2 3 4 5 6 7 8 9 10 PHX 10 09 08 07 06 05

Imagine a world without plants.
There would be no vegetables to eat.
There would be no wooden houses
to live in.
Without plants, there would be no
life on earth.

Plants are everywhere.
Some plants are big.
Some plants are small.
Some plants are weird and wacky!

Bird-of-Paradise

Is that a bird? No, it is a plant!
The bird-of-paradise is named after
its bright orange and blue flower.
The flower looks like the head of a bird.
This plant is native to South Africa.
A giant form of it grows in the state
of Hawaii in the United States.

Weird Facts

- Bird-of-paradise plants look like the flying birds-of-paradise, which are brightly colored birds.

- Seeds of the bird-of-paradise are poisonous if eaten.

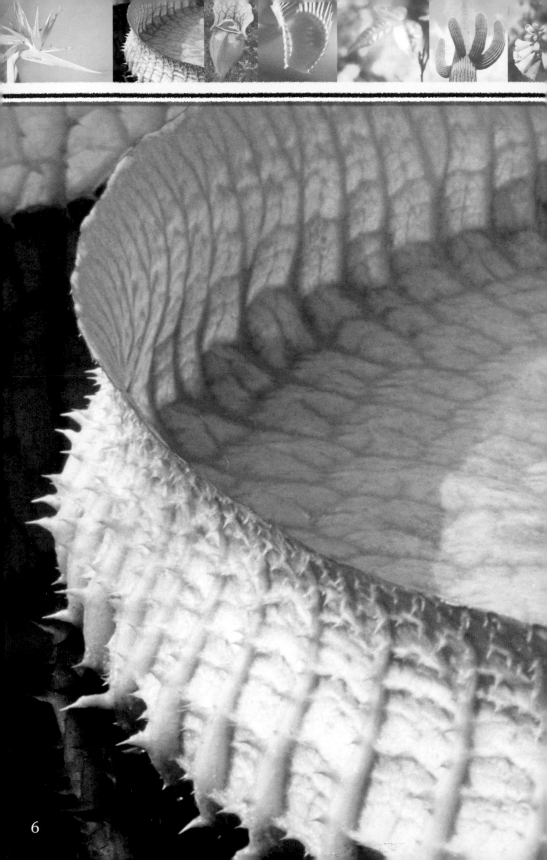

Giant Water Lily

The largest water lily in the world
is the giant water lily.
Its round leaves are seven feet wide.
A person could lie down inside of one!
The giant water lily grows in the
warm waters of the Amazon River.
This river is in South America.

Weird Facts

The giant water lily is also called the
Victoria amazonica. It was named in
1838 after Queen Victoria of England.

A giant water lily's flowers smell like
butterscotch and pineapple.

Pitcher Plant

A pitcher plant is a death trap for bugs.
It smells sweet.
The red stripes make it look like meat.
A bug flies to the plant looking for a meal.
The inside is slippery and covered
with sharp hairs.
When a bug falls inside, it cannot get out.

Weird Facts

- Pitcher plants have a drug in them that makes bugs unsteady. Bugs wobble along the rims of the plants. Then, they fall down into these deadly traps.

- Pitcher plants have clear spots on them. Bugs fly toward these sunny "windows" to escape. But they crash into the leaf and fall into the belly of the plant.

Venus Flytrap

A fly lands on leaves that look like
an open mouth.
Snap! The leaves close.
The Venus flytrap has just trapped
its food.
This plant has small hairs on its leaves.
The hairs sense when something
is there.
The edges of the leaves lock
to keep bugs inside.

Weird Facts

- Venus flytraps snap shut in one-third
  of a second.
- It takes a Venus flytrap 8-20 days
  to eat a whole bug.

Poison Ivy

Do not touch these leaves.
They are poison ivy.
Poison ivy vines climb trees,
walls, and fences.
Poison ivy also forms into a bush.
Each leaf is made of three smaller leaves.
In spring, poison ivy leaves are red.
In summer, the leaves turn
shiny and green.

Weird Facts

- The leaves of poison ivy are poisonous all year long. Touching these leaves causes red, itchy bumps.
- An allergy to poison ivy is the most common one in the United States.

Saguaro Cactus

The saguaro is the largest cactus
in the United States.
It can grow to be 60 feet tall—
as tall as a six-story building.
A saguaro cactus grows in hot,
dry deserts.
Its tall trunk and branches store water.
Sharp pins, called *spines*, cover
the saguaro cactus.

Weird Facts

- Some saguaro cacti are over 200 years old.
- Saguaro cacti can weigh ten tons—more than
  a school bus.

Foxglove

The foxglove gets its name
from its flowers.
They are shaped like the fingers
of a glove.
This purple plant looks pretty,
but it can cause harm.
A strong heart medicine is made
from foxglove leaves.
A small amount of this drug is good.
Too much of this drug can stop
a heart!

Weird Facts

- Some tales say that fairies wore foxglove blossoms as gloves. Others say that foxes put them on their paws so that they could move quietly.

- All of the foxglove plant is poisonous if eaten.

17

Bamboo

Bamboo is giant grass
with a strong stem.
Bamboo shoots grow close together
and very quickly.
Some grow three feet in one day!
Bamboo is used to make things,
like houses, shoes, fishing poles, rope,
and paper.

Weird Facts

- Layers of bamboo together are almost as strong as steel.
- Scientists think that bamboo is one of the world's earliest forms of grass.

Giant Sequoia

A giant sequoia is one of the biggest
and oldest living things on the earth.
It is a type of redwood tree.
The giant sequoia has
a very large trunk.
Most trunks are 100 feet around.
It would take a circle of almost
twenty people holding hands
to surround this giant tree!

Weird Facts

- Giant sequoias live for thousands of years.
- The largest tree in the world is a sequoia called the *General Sherman Tree*. It is over 274 feet tall and 102 feet around. It is almost five times taller than an adult oak tree.

Lichen

A lichen is a plant with no leaves,
roots, flowers, or stems.
It can live in the deep Arctic cold.
It can live in the hot desert heat.
It can live and grow on a rock!
A lichen is made of both
algae and fungi.
Algae help the lichen make food.
Fungi hold water for the lichen.

Weird Facts

- Slow-growing lichens can live to be 4,000 years old.

- For 2,000 years, doctors have used drugs made from lichens to treat lung and skin problems.

Kelp

Kelp is a large brownish-green seaweed that grows underwater.
It is found in cold waters around the world.
Many sea animals use kelp for food or shelter.
Giant kelp grows very long and very quickly.
It can grow over 300 feet in one year!

Weird Facts

- A lot of giant kelp living together forms a kelp forest. There are no trees in this forest, just kelp!

- Algin, made from kelp, is used to make ice cream, paper, and toothpaste.

Cattail

Is that a cat hiding in the grass?
No, it is a cattail!
A cattail is a wild plant.
It lives along the edges
of ponds and lakes.
It has tall, pointy green leaves.
In the spring, a cattail has
a greenish-yellow flower.
By the end of summer, the flower is
long, dark, and fuzzy like a cat's tail.

Weird Facts

- Part of the cattail flower was once used to make silk. It is still used to make bandages for cuts.

- In some parts of the world, cattails are covered with oil and set on fire. They are used as lights.

Dandelion

A bright yellow dandelion
blooms all year long.
It opens during the day
and closes up at night.
A full-grown dandelion
has white, fluffy seeds.
The word *dandelion* means
"tooth of the lion."
People think the edges of its leaves
look like a row of lion's teeth.

Weird Facts

- The early colonists brought dandelion seeds to North America. They grew dandelions for food and medicine.

- Dandelions are edible weeds! They can be cooked or used in salads.

Orchid

Many gardeners think the orchid is the most beautiful flower in the world. It grows in every color except blue! In warm places, an orchid will grow in a tree. In cool places, an orchid grows on the ground. Orchids are found in almost every type of climate except deserts.

Weird Facts

- The vanilla vine is a climbing orchid. It produces pods called *vanilla beans*. The vanilla is used in drinks and foods.

- It takes some orchid plants up to four years to recover after producing a flower.

- Birds-of-paradise belong to the banana family of plants.

- The huge white flowers of giant water lilies open for only two nights before dying.

- Tropical pitcher plants are large enough to capture small animals.

- Venus flytraps can count to two! The trigger hairs on the leaves must be touched twice before the plant will close.

- Oil from poison ivy stays active on clothing for a whole year.

- Saguaro (sə-gwär´-ō) cacti have ridges and grooves that expand and contract like an accordion to adjust to the amount of stored water.

- If eaten, two to four foxglove leaves can kill an adult human.

- Some bamboo can grow 120 feet tall.

- The bark on a giant sequoia (sĭ- kwoi´-ə) tree can be over a foot thick!

- Lichen (lī´-kən) can produce an acid that is strong enough to break apart rock.

- Giant kelp grows to be over 300 feet, as long as a football field.

- Cattail pollen is used as tinder for fires. It is extremely flammable.

- It is said that dandelions are more healthful to eat than spinach or broccoli.

- There are over 5,000 species of orchids, but none of them are blue.